THE COMING OF CHRIST

THE COMING OF CHRIST

FOUR BROADCAST ADDRESSES
FOR THE SEASON OF ADVENT

BY

C. H. DODD

*formerly Norris-Hulse Professor of Divinity
in the University of Cambridge*

CAMBRIDGE
AT THE UNIVERSITY PRESS
1954

CAMBRIDGE UNIVERSITY PRESS
Cambridge, New York, Melbourne, Madrid, Cape Town, Singapore, São Paulo, Delhi

Cambridge University Press
The Edinburgh Building, Cambridge CB2 8RU, UK

Published in the United States of America by Cambridge University Press, New York

www.cambridge.org
Information on this title: www.cambridge.org/9780521070454

First edition 1951
Second edition 1954
This digitally printed version 2008

A catalogue record for this publication is available from the British Library

ISBN 978-0-521-07045-4 hardback
ISBN 978-0-521-09778-9 paperback

PREFACE

This book consists of four addresses broadcast in
the Home Service of the British Broadcasting
Corporation, on the four Sundays in Advent, 1950.
They have been printed virtually as delivered
through the microphone, with only the necessary
minimum of verbal alteration.

C. H. D.

Cambridge, January 1951

CONTENTS

I

THE PROMISE OF HIS COMING

THE period immediately before Christmas is known in the Church calendar as the season of Advent, the word 'advent' meaning a coming, or an arrival. The theme of Advent is the coming of Christ into the world. We are accustomed to use that expression in two different senses, which seem to run into one another. On the one hand, we think of the coming of Christ as a babe at Christmas, and on the other hand we think of a more mysterious coming, which is often called His 'second advent'. All through these weeks we are in a mood of expectancy. On one side of it our expectation will be fulfilled when Christmas comes, and we are able to sing: 'Christians, awake! Salute the happy morn, Whereon the Saviour of mankind was born.' But what about that other expectation?

'He shall come again with glory to judge both the living and the dead.' In those words the whole Christian world confesses its faith. They are words that stir the imagination, and speak to

1

something lying very deep in us. But what precisely do we mean by them? How does it fit into our general outlook on life and the world in the twentieth century?

We must begin by looking at the New Testament, to see if we can form any clear idea of what was in the minds of the early Christian teachers who handed down this belief to later ages. 'The promise of His coming' was for them all a matter of profound conviction; but they speak variously, and often obscurely, about the manner of the coming, its time and place, and what is to follow. Perhaps they differ less than might appear. They are in any case not setting out to give precise specifications in advance of what is going to happen, like history written in reverse. They are hinting, through images and symbols, at truths which cannot be baldly stated in plain prose. Symbolism is fluid, and images change as one aspect or another of the truth comes into view. So we need not be in the least surprised if one writer speaks of Christ coming down on a cloud, and another speaks of Him riding a white horse at the head of the armies of heaven. They are not speaking of different things.

The imagery was created by poets, some of whose works are in the Old Testament, especially in the Psalms, the Book of Job, and parts of the prophetical books. These biblical writers have one over-riding theme: the majesty of God. Everything that is awe-inspiring in nature speaks to them of His majesty: great mountains, earthquakes, eclipses of the sun and moon, shooting meteors, storms at sea, and the uncanny calm that sometimes succeeds a storm: 'He maketh the storm a calm, so that the waves are still.' The prophets often spoke of a great Day to come, when God would make His power and righteousness known to all nations; and they turned the same time-honoured symbolism to account. It meets us again in the New Testament:

'There shall be signs in sun and moon and stars, and upon the earth distress of nations in perplexity for the roaring of the sea and the billows.' 'The sun shall be darkened and the moon shall not give her light, and the stars shall fall out of the sky, and the powers that are in the heavens shall be shaken. And then shall they see the Son of Man coming in clouds with great power and glory.'

It would be intolerable to take such language with a prosaic literalness. It is addressed to the imagination, and read with imagination it gives a key to what the coming of Christ meant to the first Christians. It was the final disclosure of the power and righteousness of God, and the end of history as we know it. It was the 'one divine event to which the whole creation moves'.

But not a 'far-off divine event'; not far off at all. Most of them were persuaded it would happen very soon. It might happen any day. They had to be on the alert; everything was uncertain, except the one certainty: the Lord would come.

Since this whole present scheme of things (they thought) could not be relied on to hold together for any appreciable time, they sat loose to it. And that detachment bred a sense of freedom and independence. Because they had no stake in the existing order, they were able to set about creating a new kind of society, on a new ethical basis. Paradoxically, because they thought there was not going to be any more history, they made history.

They believed that the Last Judgment was so near that they were living practically in its presence; and that was a mighty stimulant to the conscience. At the same time it made them willing to let the Almighty manage His own business; and in particular it saved them from the temptation to forestall His judgment on their fellow-men. 'Pass no judgment before the time', wrote Paul, 'until the Lord comes.' It was not their business to put other people right. They had

4

enough to do, and God had the situation well in hand.

But the most striking thing about the early Christians was their astonishing confidence in the face of overwhelming opposition. The Church was a minority movement, with every kind of power in the world against it. But they were convinced that all this power was already crumbling away. They knew it, and soon (they thought) everyone would know it. So they refused to be intimidated.

In giving this very summary sketch of the outlook of an early Christian I have left out a most important fact. These people did not simply expect a great 'divine event'; they expected the coming of Jesus Christ, whom they knew. It was not just a Last Judgment they expected. It was the judgment of Christ; and they knew what standards He judged by, and how His judgment passed into a forgiveness that set a man up again. The victory they counted on was the victory of Christ—the same who had preached the Sermon on the Mount, befriended publicans and sinners, and sacrificed His life for love of the human race. The Christian hope might be expressed in fantastic imagery, but it was based on no fantasy, but upon known facts about a known person, whose known character and achievement gave a clear stamp to the picture of what was to come. The really distinctive thing about the early Christian outlook was not so much the expectation of something that was going to happen, as the understanding of what had happened: Christ's life, teaching and death, in history.

This became very important when the expectation of His early return proved an illusion. The Church was mistaken about the date of the great event. At first they had looked for it almost any day. During the first century events occurred from time to time which raised hopes that it was at hand; but they were always disappointed, as similar hopes have been disappointed many times since. When a century had passed after the death of Jesus, one of the later writers of the New Testament observed that 'one day is with the Lord as a thousand years, and a thousand years as one day'; as much as to say, ordinary time-measurements do not apply; it may be thousands of years before the Lord comes; even so, He comes soon. But perhaps there is more to it than that. If the early Christians were mistaken about the date, perhaps they were mistaken in trying to fix a date at all. Perhaps the coming of Christ is dateless, because it lies outside our system of time-reckoning altogether.

It might have been expected that when the

Church proved to have been mistaken on such an important point, its faith would have been shaken to its foundations, and its mission to the world discredited. But not at all. The surprising thing is that the period in which the first expectation of Christ's early return faded away was a great period in the history of the Church; a period in which it developed and consolidated its beliefs, endured persecution heroically, and grew rapidly in numbers. Evidently the mistake about the date did not touch the substance of the Christian hope. How was this? I believe the answer is that, through the disappointment of the hopes they had formed, they woke to something they had always known, but until then had not fully appreciated: the thing *had happened*; Christ had come. All these years they had been living on that fact, while they supposed their faith hung upon the prospect of His second coming. Now it came home to them: God's victory was won; Christ had won it; and they already shared in it. So they made the necessary readjustments in their thought without for a moment losing grip.

That did not mean that they gave up the hope of another coming of Christ. They were realists. They knew that God's enemies were still strongly entrenched in their positions, and there were many battles still to fight. God's victory was won; it was yet to win. Both things were true. So the Christian life became a tension between realisation and expectation. After all, even in our daily prayer we say: 'Thy kingdom come...For thine is the kingdom, for ever.' The kingdom is still to come, and yet it is present, always; and that is why we have confidence in praying for its coming. It may be a paradox, but this tension has been a great strength to the Christian religion. So it seems we must say that for the early Church the coming of Christ was both present and future, both at once. You could not say that of any ordinary event in history. But, as I suggested before, the coming of Christ is an event that lies outside our system of time-reckoning. It has no date; and so through the whole season of Advent we can speak of the coming of Christ, meaning both His birth into the world a long time ago, and the unimaginable fullness of His coming; and speak of both as if they lay just round the corner.

The tension between realisation and expectation found moving expression in the worship of the early Church. The first Christians were accustomed to meet regularly and often to take a meal together in memory of Jesus. At such a meal

He had taken leave of them on the evening before His death. They made the memory vivid by repeating what He had said and done on that never-to-be-forgotten occasion. Thus the facts of His life and death became more than a memory: a present experience. Then they prayed together. One of the prayers they used on such occasions has come down to us from the very earliest days in the Aramaic speech which was native to Jesus and His first disciples. It consists of two words: 'Lord, come!' (*Marana tha*). If we use our imagination to enter with sympathy into the scene, those words, in their extreme simplicity, bear witness to the spirit of tense expectancy in which they came together. But they did not stop at that. They knew that a Presence was there, unseen and unheard, but real: the Lord had come to them. 'He was known to them in the breaking of bread.' Expectation passed into realisation. And realisation in turn kindled fresh expectancy. For the more deeply they appreciated what they had already received, the more clearly they knew that there is on earth nothing complete—there is always more to hope for. Thus both the urgency and the immediacy of the early hope, which might have seemed lost when the date of the great event was postponed indefinitely, were restored, and the permanent rhythm of the Christian faith was established.

If you are accustomed to go to church, you will of course recognise that I have been describing an early form of the service which is still the centre of Christian worship—whether we call it the Lord's Supper or the Mass, the Eucharist or Holy Communion. I have drawn your attention to it because I believe it is here that we must look for a key to the paradox of a coming of Christ which is past, present and future all in one. It is perhaps not possible to put the truth into plain logical speech, except within narrow limits. It may be suggested, as we have seen, by symbols and images. But it may best be grasped in the act of worship.

II

CHRIST IN THE GOSPELS

So far I have tried to trace and explain the main lines of early Christian belief about what is called the 'second coming' of Christ. Now I want to raise the even more important question: What did Jesus Christ Himself teach about it? The passages on this subject in the Gospels are certainly not easy to understand. They have been endlessly discussed, and there is still room for difference of opinion. I certainly cannot profess to give an authoritative solution. But I shall try to develop one line of interpretation which has seemed to me, in the course of many years' study of the New Testament, to be worth following.

I start by asking: What is the main trend of the teaching of Jesus, looked at broadly, in its historical setting as the Gospels give it? One thing is un-mistakable. All through the story there is a sense of crisis. Momentous events are in process. Quick decisions are called for. A conflict is afoot, working up swiftly to a head. The climax comes in the tragedy of Good Friday, soon succeeded by the

11   2-2

triumph of Easter Day. That is the setting for the teaching of Jesus. It is teaching for a crisis. That is why so many of the parables are variations on a single plot: a long-continued process comes suddenly to a head, and something drastic happens. The servants of a great household are sitting up for the absent master. They mark the tedious passage of the hours, from evening to midnight, from midnight to cockcrow, from cockcrow to dawn, and nothing happens. Then suddenly the master is there. If they were ready, well and good; if not, no excuses are accepted. How many stories there are in this vein—stories about 'zero-hour'. The moral is, 'Be ready!' Then what was 'zero-hour' in real life and who were the people who had to be ready?

The answer that is mostly given is that the 'zero-hour' of the parables is the second coming of Christ. The truth that there is in that answer I shall come to presently. But surely it is no event in the distant future that they envisage. The note of urgency sounds too insistently. Those very people whom Jesus addressed, at that very time, were confronted with the moment of decision. It was they to whom the warning was addressed: 'Be ready!'

Jesus had begun His work, we are told, by

announcing that a crisis had arrived: 'The time is fulfilled; the kingdom of God is upon you.' He taught His followers to recognise in the swiftly moving events in which they were caught up the characteristic signs of the great 'Day of the Lord'. He saw signs of it even in the bitter opposition He aroused and in the very catastrophe that threatened. He spoke of the catastrophe in terms which at any rate made it clear that it was no merely personal tragedy, but the most momentous thing that had ever happened, for all mankind. As it drew near, He warned His followers with increasing urgency, as He had already warned them in many parables, to be on the alert for 'zero-hour', so that they might not be taken unprepared by the sudden ordeal. 'What I say to you I say to all: watch!' 'Watch and pray, that you enter not into temptation.' As He uttered that warning for the last time, His enemies were already at the gate of the garden where He had taken refuge with His friends, and the next moment the trial was upon them. They were not ready. The parables of 'zero-hour', surely, in their first intention, were directed to this immediate contingency.

But beyond the catastrophe Jesus had taught them to look to final triumph. Sometimes He spoke of rising from the dead; sometimes, in more traditional language, of 'the kingdom of God come with power'; and sometimes He used that ancient symbol of the ultimate victory of the good cause, 'the Son of Man coming with the clouds of heaven'. What I am suggesting is that in their first intention all these mean the same thing: immediate victory out of apparent defeat. That was what Jesus promised. What happened was that He shortly returned, alive after death, invested with the power and glory of another world; He rallied His discredited followers, conveyed to them the power of His Spirit, and let them loose on the world; and so a new era began: the kingdom of Christ on earth. And that is what He said would happen.

That was the coming of Christ in history. As interpreted by Jesus Himself, His total career on earth was the crisis in which the long awaited kingdom of God came upon men. The crisis began when He started His ministry; it was complete when He returned from death. The thing had happened. They needed no longer to say, 'the Son of Man will come'; He had come; He was sitting on the throne of His glory, the invisible King of mankind. That is the faith of the New Testament; it has been the faith of the Church all through; and it has the warrant of Christ's own teaching.

14

Whatever else may be in prospect, Christ has come. That is the most important thing. At Christmas time we shall be proclaiming the fact with every token of rejoicing.

But that is not the whole truth about what Christ taught. There are some mysterious sayings about the coming of the Son of Man which I have passed over too lightly. There are passages where we are told that before He comes there will be a breakdown of the physical universe. I said before that it would be absurd to take literally the language about the darkened sun and falling stars. All the same, we cannot easily dismiss the impression that the final scene is laid where the world of space, time and matter is no longer in the picture. It is in no world of time and space that the nations of the dead, as well as the living, stand before Christ for judgment, as we are told they will. And there is that strange thing that Jesus is reported to have said at His trial before the High Priest: 'You shall see the Son of Man seated at the right hand of the Almighty.' Make all the allowance we may for symbolic language, can we give any meaning to such a statement unless we think of another world than this? I hesitate ever to press any single saying, where all are so enigmatic; but surely the total impression is that the

15

forecasts of a coming of Christ in history (fulfilled in His resurrection) are balanced by forecasts of a coming beyond history: definitely, I should say, *beyond* history, and not as a further event *in* history, not even the last event.

And now comes a really difficult question. Did Jesus Christ, then, teach, as some of His followers seem to have thought, that almost immediately after His resurrection history would be wound up and the world come to an end? Of course it did not do so. Then was Jesus mistaken on this point? There are Christian scholars who think He was. They point out that, according to the Gospels, He actually confessed that He was ignorant about the time of His second coming: 'Of that day and hour no one knows, not the angels, not even the Son, but only the Father.' And they urge that the very fact that He 'was made man' means that He accepted some human limitations of knowledge; which is true. And so, drawing what seems the logical inference from some of the sayings I have referred to, they suppose that He contemplated His own second coming as the immediate conclusion of the whole process: ministry in Galilee, conflict in Jerusalem, crucifixion, resurrection, and then—the end of the world.

But there is weighty evidence that points in a

different direction. The Gospels contain a number
of forecasts of historical events, spread over a
considerable period. Jesus is said to have foretold
a time of troubles after His departure, including
the downfall of Jerusalem and the ruin of the
temple. No doubt such forecasts may have been
made more precise and explicit in the light of what
happened afterwards; but we simply cannot write
them all off as 'prophecies after the event'. In
particular, I cannot resist the evidence that He
saw the destined destruction of the temple at
Jerusalem in a quite special relation to His own
coming, since it marked dramatically the close of
the old era in religion, to make way for the new.
In short, I see no reason to doubt that Jesus did
prepare His disciples for a time of troubles, and
give them guidance how to meet it. Consequently
He must have contemplated a further period of
history after His departure.

In any case—and this is still more significant—
a great part of the teaching of Jesus is concerned
with human conduct, and with conduct in society
(social ethics, as we say). It consequently pre-
supposes the continuance of human society much
as we know it. Think of the Sermon on the Mount.
This is not legislation for an ideal world, for it
contemplates a state of society where you may be

struck on the cheek or have your cloak stolen. And it is not in the least plausible to suggest that it is no more than 'interim ethics', designed for a very short period before history is wound up. It is too universal, too permanent.

So we seem to be left with several groups of sayings which on the face of them point in different directions. Sometimes, it seems, they associate the coming of the Son of Man in glory, the kingdom of God, and the Last Judgment, with the historical ministry of Jesus Christ; sometimes they associate it with historical crises yet to come; and sometimes with that which lies beyond all history, in another world than this.

I put it to you that He meant all these, and all at once. Does that sound very far-fetched? Let me remind you that poets very often use language with just such a double meaning; one meaning on the surface, another beneath the surface. This doubleness of meaning is not ambiguity or confusion of thought. That is the way poets see life; not all on one level, but depth below depth; and I had rather take their word than most people's. The human mind of Jesus Christ was a poet's mind. That stands out on every page of the Gospels. Where others saw only incidents in the career of a rustic prophet who came to a sad end,

He saw the great Day of the Lord; not only saw it, but acted it out. He saw that Day come, in the brief spell when He worked and suffered in Palestine. He saw it extended into history yet to be. He saw it extended into the world beyond history, where alone the kingdom of God can be perfectly revealed. And yet it was *there*, really and actually. The Day had come.

Some of the early Christians understood this clearly. In the Fourth Gospel John makes Jesus say, just before His death: '*Now* is the judgment of this world'—the Last Judgment, he means; and John was not mistaken. Others took to themselves the parables of 'zero-hour', and now that the original emergency was long past, they found a new application of that stern warning, 'Be ready'; for who knew in what sort of emergency the Lord would come again, or when? And *they* were not mistaken. Some early Jewish Christians, who witnessed the horrors of the war in which Jerusalem fell, said (and we can understand their feelings) 'It is the end of the world'; and they took comfort from the words of the Lord; 'When these things begin to come to pass, look up, and lift up your heads, for your redemption draws near.' And *they* were not mistaken, even though the Lord did not come in the way they imagined.

He did come again, through those very calamities, to detach them from their past, and to challenge them to enter on more spacious ways.

And *we* in turn shall not be mistaken if, while we turn our minds to the coming of Christ 1950 years ago, we also expect Him to come in this menacing situation to which history has brought us. In and through what is now happening, He may call us to some decisive new departure. If we are watchful to 'discern the signs of the times', as He told His disciples to be, we shall be ready to respond to unexpected challenges. And finally, we shall not mistake His intention if we always bear in mind that this world is a temporary and provisional affair. It will pass, and there will be nothing between us and Him.

III

THE LORD OF HISTORY

I F we reflect on human life in this world, I suppose the most obvious thing about it is that it has its limitations. We are free beings, no doubt. We are free to choose among the things that are possible. We are not free to choose between the possible and the impossible. Our power to do things is bounded by the laws of nature, including our own nature; and we cannot alter them. Our field of knowledge is bounded. And in fact our whole existence on earth lies inside the boundary of time—it lasts just so long and no longer. It has a beginning and an end. Birth and death are frontier-posts by which we enter and leave this limited realm; and the frontier control is strict.

Most of our living and thinking are done safely within the boundary. We are born; we go to school; we find a job; we marry and have children and bring them up as best we can; and then we grow old. A fortunate and well-planned life is supposed to leave you with enough to live on, children happily settled, a fund of memories of

21

which at least a fair proportion are pleasant to dwell on, and at the end a peaceful decline, and so to sleep. All very well indeed, and well inside the boundary. Yet even so I think it is an exceptionally tough-minded creature, however fortunate in life, who is not sometimes vaguely troubled about that final drop of the curtain. Certainly, most of us are painfully reminded from time to time of our limitations. We find ourselves thwarted by circumstances over which we have no control. We resent not being able to foresee what is coming (and that is why people in our time turn to astrology). And we simply hate having to face the truth that death is a real frontier-post.

It is not only that you and I and the next man are thus limited. The human race as a whole is shut up within the boundary. Its life on earth began and will end. There is no substance in the idea that though individuals die the race is immortal. There is no more substance in the idea that man has all knowledge and all power within his grasp, if only he can find the right techniques; and that given time he will find them. Those ideas are little better than compensations in fantasy for our painful sense of limitation.

True wisdom for man is to acknowledge his limitations. Instead of trying to ignore the boundary, our desire should be to understand it. Is it, for example, simply the point at which our knowledge, our powers, and ultimately our ability to go on living at all, come to a stop, because there just isn't anything more? Or is it that a malignant fate sets out to thwart us? Few people, I suppose, hold that as a serious view of life, but most of us sometimes behave as if we did, when things do not go to our liking. The answers we find to such questions as these will have considerable effect on the spirit in which we accept our experiences, and make our plans, inside the boundary.

The answer that religion gives is plain: human existence on earth is bounded by the decree of almighty God. The boundary is not just a dead end. It is not a stone wall or an iron curtain. It is alive. It is nothing else than the active power of the Creator, at work shaping the creation to His plan. Where human knowledge fails, the eternal Wisdom takes charge. Where we come to the end of our own powers, we fall into the hands of the Almighty. When each individual person reaches the frontier post of death, he steps into the presence of the Eternal. And when in due course history ends, and the human race perishes from this planet, it will encounter God.

That is what religion teaches. Any view of life

that is religious in any sense must say at least so
much. But when a Christian says the word 'God',
he is thinking of God in Christ, and that makes a
distinction. For us, God is not simply the maker
of all things, or the ultimate power. He is all
that; but He is also the God who revealed Himself
in a crucial passage of recorded history, and in the
person of its chief actor. From that we know that
the Power that hems us in is not only perfectly
wise, but completely good; and He wishes us well.
It is neither indifference nor ill will that bounds
our life, but in the last resort the love of God.
And *this* God meets us at the frontier, where the
life of our race reaches its term: God in Christ.

That is how I understand the mysterious
language of the Gospels about the final coming
of the Son of Man. Unlike His first coming, it
is not an event *in* history. It is the point at which
all history is taken up into the larger whole of
God's eternal purpose. It is the point at which
not only the latest achievements of the race find
fulfilment, but its forgotten struggles, and even
its failures. And the forgotten people, whose
struggles never showed any success, will find their
fulfilment too. Many of our human estimates of
success and failure will be reversed; for we shall
see our lives, and the total life of mankind, as

God sees it. And what even the finest of human efforts failed to achieve, even in the long lapse of centuries, will be supplied out of the fullness of God—God in Christ.

But that will not be the first time the history of mankind has had direct contact with God in Christ. We speak of it as His *second* coming; and that should keep us in mind that there was a first. At that one point, God in Christ made Himself into a character in history. He came inside the boundary, and accepted our limitations. By living as a man among men, He brought to light the true values which history is meant to serve, and the goals at which it is meant to aim. Inevitably, the false values and aims of men defined themselves in opposition; and so a conflict developed. Such conflict is a characteristic feature of history; always has been, and probably always will be. The opposition to Jesus Christ had behind it such forces as a political ambition, mistaken religious zeal, personal and class prejudice, and the like; familiar enough to all observers of history, past and present. The evil in them was mixed up with specious and even praiseworthy motives, just as it is in history as we know it. By the way He faced the opposition, Christ showed up the forces behind it for what they truly were—powers destructive of human life as God designed it; powers of death. In the upshot, He voluntarily put Himself under death and destruction, and by doing so triumphed over them, and reaffirmed life—life absolute and eternal—as what God intends for man.

That is a piece of real history. It is history made out of the same stuff as the history we know. But it was shaped by an incursion from beyond the boundary, and it worked itself out to a conclusion. If we have in any measure understood it, we are at the centre of what history really means. This is the meaning that will be revealed when the whole plot has been worked out.

It has become a matter of real concern to our generation to have some understanding of our situation in history. We live at a time when the stream is rushing headlong through the rapids, and sweeping us along; and there seems to be little we can do about it. Certainly we can cherish no illusion that we shall be allowed to work out our personal plans secure from interference from events in the great world. We should like to know whether the stream is getting anywhere with us. In other words, is there any meaning or purpose in history; and if so, have our individual lives any significant place in it?

When I was young, the belief in progress was there to give us a sense that life and effort were worth while. Popular authors wrote imaginatively about the Utopia of the future, and encouraged us to think of 'men like gods' walking proudly upon an earthly scene where everything was at last brought to perfection. In recent years several eminent writers have given us *their* picture of the future. There is not much Utopia about it. Often it is quite revolting. If that is what it is all coming to, we are tempted to say, what is the good of it? History will have failed. Fortunately, these gloomy vaticinations need not be taken any more seriously than their over-optimistic predecessors. All experience shows that the ability of mankind to foresee the remoter results of its actions is strictly limited. Really, we have no idea how things will develop.

Meanwhile, through all these fluctuations of thought, from one extreme to the other, the Christian Gospel has not altered. It may be that we have not always been sufficiently aware that it does not address itself only to the salvation of individual men and women, but is concerned with the destiny of mankind. This concern is especially distinct in all that it has to say about Christ's final coming. Of course, it does apply individually.

Singly we must pass the last frontier when our time is up. In a real sense that is the moment when Christ comes again for each of us. But everywhere in the New Testament it is mankind corporately that is in view when Christ is contemplated coming in glory 'to judge the living and the dead'. That expression means the whole human race: all whose lives and actions make up the course of history, past, present, and future.

Christianity does not provide materials for constructing the course of history yet to come. It offers us no Utopia on earth. But it does assure us what the final meaning of it all is. Mystery remains; but there is no dark secret to be sprung on us. There is nothing awaiting us which could contradict what Christ disclosed at His first coming. To learn about His second coming we are not left to pore over dubious symbols, or to speculate beyond the allotted limits of human experience. We have to read the Gospels, dig deep into their story, and see what history looks like in the light of it, and what our part in it all is.

Here we may learn to recognise, among the perplexities of our existence, which courses of action will prove themselves to have been worth while, when all is summed up, and which are mere vanity and will pass into nothingness. They will be judged—and indeed are being judged now—by the standards Christ set up. We may learn what was His ideal for human life. That ideal is not only permanently applicable; but, because it represents the Creator's own design for His creatures, we know that it will in the end be attained, however strange, and often unpromising, the course we travel to reach it. Once again, from what Christ said and did, still more from what He was, we learn what it concerns us to know about the true and final relation between man and his Maker; and that is in the last resort the key to everything. And finally, we learn from His earthly adventure, and what came of it, the true nature of the last frontier-post, and who it is that awaits us there. More than that we do not need to know.

FOURTH SUNDAY IN ADVENT

(CHRISTMAS EVE, 1950)

FROM ADVENT TO CHRISTMAS

WHEN we were children, we used to count the days to Christmas. When Christmas Eve came, the suspense was almost too great to bear. Christmas Eve has come again. It is to be hoped that we are still children enough to feel some thrill of expectation. But what is it that we expect from to-morrow's festival—as a religious festival, I mean, a Christian festival?

On Christmas Day we commemorate an important event that happened a long time ago. After it happened, many people found in it the fulfilment of hopes and aspirations that had been cherished for centuries past. To recollect these ancient hopes gives point to the Christmas message. That is one reason why it is the custom in most churches to read at this season certain passages from the prophetical books of the Old Testament; passages which give expression, in sublime poetry, to these age-old and universal longings of the human heart. They dwell on such themes as justice, freedom and truth, wisdom needed for our guidance in a perplexing world, law to bring order out of disorder, authority that all men will recognise freely, and, above all, peace on earth. If we can put ourselves in the place of those generations before Christ, and feel their need, and the tenseness of their longing, it brings us into the mood of expectancy, and prepares us to hear the note of triumph when Christ's birth is proclaimed.

But is that all? Is it just a matter of working up the excitement to give point to the celebration? I think not. The fact is that we are not merely imagining ourselves to be where those people were in the centuries 'B.C.'. In a real sense we *are* where they were; still awaiting our salvation. We are certainly no strangers to the kind of experiences which stirred those ancient longings. These people had been through times of social unrest and strife of classes, a decline of national morale, the wearing threat of war, which at last broke out; then a series of military reverses ending in total defeat, the sight of their capital city destroyed by enemy action, and the miserable lot of displaced persons in unfriendly countries. These were the conditions that gave rise to those desperate appeals to the unseen Power ('Oh, that

31

Thou wouldst rend the heavens and come down') and finally to those confident promises of the coming of a Saviour. But is there one single item in that catalogue which has not been part of the destiny of our generation? No doubt in this country we have been spared the worst (so far); but we cannot detach ourselves from the common lot; and no one of us can contract out of the consequences, material or spiritual—as we all know. We are living through one of the recurrent crises of history that offer a special challenge to the spirit of man.

How shall we respond to it? By helpless resignation? Or by 'wishful thinking'? Or shall we hope for the best and prepare for the worst, grit our teeth and see it through? That is the response this nation has given before now; and let us hope we are still capable of it. The question is, has the Christian faith anything to add to this? I believe it has. It has 'the promise of His coming'; and not only that final coming that lies beyond history, but a coming into *this* situation— this Christmas, it may be.

The thing that Christianity has to say to us becomes relevant, when once we have made up our minds that the real problem of our time is a moral and spiritual problem. The advances and withdrawals of armies, diplomatic moves, economic plans, and all the rest, are on the level of symptoms. The real conflict is on the field of the spirit.

> They cease not fighting, East and West,
> On the marches of my breast.

The decision will be made in the minds and hearts of countless men and women in all countries. When I speak, therefore, of our critical situation, I am thinking primarily of a crisis of the spirit of man in our time. As this crisis is resolved, one way or another, it will decide the outward course of history in the next period. It is to the inner crisis that the Christian Gospel is addressed, and, in particular, the Christmas message is addressed.

Suppose at such a time as this some exceptionally clear-sighted and well-informed observer were to reckon up the various factors in the situation. Suppose he were not only able to assess material resources, but even to get down to the intangibles, and estimate the strength of the ideals and motives by which men and nations are guided, and the moral energy they command. We are, of course, supposing an impossibility; but just suppose it. He might then produce a reasonably accurate forecast of the way things are going. But then suppose some genuinely new factor came in—something that could not have been allowed for, because it was not there before at all. The whole process would be thrown into a different gear. And (since we are indulging in suppositions) suppose that in our present critical situation the new factor were one making for the healing of our troubles, then there would indeed be a ground of hope, and a stimulus to action, that would have nothing to do with 'wishful thinking'.

That is precisely what our Christian faith assures us is in fact true. When Christ came into the world 1950 years ago, something quite new entered history, from beyond the frontier of human existence, and the whole outlook for mankind in this world was permanently altered. It put history into a new gear. As we have already seen, what came to earth then was final and decisive for the whole meaning and purpose of human existence, and we shall meet it again when history has been wound up.

But we do not have to wait until then. At the last frontier-post we shall encounter God in Christ; but meanwhile He keeps watch all along the boundary that limits our life on earth, and everywhere His power presses in upon us, from beyond the frontier. History is always open to

His approach. Only there seem to be certain crises in history, as there are in the experience of many individual people, when He comes with power, and there is unmistakably a new factor in the situation to be reckoned with. I believe the period we are living through is such a crisis. It certainly looks as if the course of events were shaping towards a decision, one way or the other. We wait anxiously upon developments. Meanwhile, it is an open possibility that in our time the power from beyond the frontier will intervene and upset all our calculations.

If we may judge from precedent, it is unlikely that any such intervention will be at all spectacular. When Christ was born, the general public took no notice. But the thing had happened, and its consequences became apparent. Any such intervention may be as little like anything we could forecast as was the coming of Christ 1950 years ago; and perhaps as little welcome, until we have understood. It would be going beyond the book to predict any particular issue out of our present historical predicament such as we ourselves might choose. There is no promise of immediate success for any cause we may have at heart. Christ's own victory came through defeat and death. But it *was* victory, though it took

faith to recognise it at the time; and history cor-
roborated it. The ways in which God in Christ
comes are various, and they are not obvious. That
is the point of the repeated warnings to watch
and be ready.

Yet there is a fundamental pattern of all Christ's
comings. It is the pattern that appears in the
Gospels. His impact upon a historical situation
begins by arresting men with a sense of God's
judgment on their ways. In our present crisis
I do not see how we can avoid that sense of
judgment, or exempt ourselves from it. In the
Gospels, those who found themselves judged in
the presence of Christ, and got no further, went
away sorrowful and angry, and there for them
the story ended. But if men acknowledged that
His judgment upon them was true, and put their
consciences under it, so that they lost taste for
their former ways, then they found that judgment
passed into forgiveness, and forgiveness proved
a fresh beginning. Out of it came that renewal
of human life which was Christ's historical
achievement; and there is no reason why we may
not look for such renewal in our own time.

In the familiar Christmas story, after the
momentous announcement is made to the shep-
herds, they are told: 'This shall be the sign to you:

you shall find a babe wrapped in swaddling bands and lying in a manger.' The sign is appropriate: a new-born child, exposed to view in utter simplicity, so that nothing is to be seen but the new life that has come into the world. Other religions have used the symbol of the Birth of the Child; no symbol could more powerfully represent the idea of a new beginning. But in Christianity the symbol is fact. The Child *was* born, and 'the world's great age begins anew'.

The Gospels lay stress on the response, positive or negative, that men made to Christ when He came; it was an essential part of His total impact on history; and our response will be an essential part of His impact on our present situation. God's gifts are never given like presents in a Christmas stocking. They are always challenges that we must take up. And yet, it is not we who start anything. Behind our repentance, our faith, our good resolutions, is the prior fact that God in Christ comes. He comes with a power and reality that do not depend on us. History attests His power to free men from their past and to start new things. He has done it before and He can do it again. That is our confidence. It is anchored in historical fact, which nothing can alter. It is anchored also in the timeless truth that He is

Lord of history, and will appear as such when all is over. We have His word for it, and it is witnessed by faith—which is, after all, our only means of knowing *ultimate* truths, in any field of knowledge. Hanging upon these two fixed points is our assurance that Christ comes to us in our immediate situation. What we await tomorrow is not simply the commemoration of the birth of Christ long ago; it is also the opportunity of welcoming Him now. I should like to think that many of us, worried as we are by the news of public dangers and distresses, hard hit as some of us are in our private lives, are turning our anxiety into a longing, a prayer and a hope that Christ will come into this menacing situation. If we have done so, then these weeks of Advent will have been a time of well-justified and mounting expectation, and we stand on the threshold of great things.

I am going to finish by quoting a few sentences which gather up these hopes and prayers. They will be familiar to some of you, strange to others. They will have been said or sung in innumerable churches all over the Christian world in these last days of preparation for Christmas; for they are part of the ancient services for the season of Advent. Here they are:

O Wisdom, which camest forth out of the mouth of the Most High, reaching from world's end to world's end, mightily and sweetly ordering all things: come, and teach us the way of prudence.

O Lord, and Leader of the house of Israel, who didst appear to Moses in the flame of a burning bush, and gavest him the Law on Sinai: come, and deliver us with outstretched arm.

O Root of Jesse, who standest for an ensign of the peoples, before whom kings fall silent, unto whom the nations shall make entreaty: come and deliver us, and tarry not.

O Key of David, and Sceptre of the house of Israel, who openest and none shutteth, who shuttest and none openeth: come, and bring the prisoner out of the prison-house.

O Dayspring, the Splendour of everlasting light and Sun of righteousness: come, and enlighten them that sit in darkness and the shadow of death.

O King of the nations and their desire, the corner-stone that maketh both one: come, and save mankind whom thou didst form of clay.

O Emmanuel—God with us—our King and Law-giver, the hope of the nations and their salvation: come and save us, O Lord our God.

To all these aspirations of the human heart there is one answer: 'Christ is born. O come, let us adore Him.'

For EU product safety concerns, contact us at Calle de José Abascal, 56–1°,
28003 Madrid, Spain or eugpsr@cambridge.org.

www.ingramcontent.com/pod-product-compliance
Ingram Content Group UK Ltd.
Pitfield, Milton Keynes, MK11 3LW, UK
UKHW012334130625
459647UK00009B/278